JOHN MERRILL'S
CHARNWOOD
FOREST
CHALLENGE WALK

by

John N. Merrill

Maps and photographs by John N. Merrill

Trail Crest Publications Ltd.,
- "from footprint to finished book".

1992

1

TRAIL CREST
PUBLICATIONS
Ltd.,
WINSTER,
MATLOCK,
DERBYSHIRE.
DE4 2DQ

 Winster (0629) 650454
Winster (0629) 650416

Concieved, edited, typeset, designed, paged, marketed and distributed by John N. Merrill.

© Text and routes - John N. Merrill 1992.
© Maps - John N. Merrill 1992.
© Photographs - John N. Merrill 1992.

First Published - JULY 1992.

ISBN 0 907496 64 4

U.S.A.
office -
P.O.Box 124.
Santa Rosa,
New Mexico.
88435
U.S.A.

Please note : The maps in this guide are purely illustrative. You are encouraged to walk with the appropriate Ordnance Survey map as detailed for each walk.

Meticulous research has been undertaken to ensure that this publication is highly accurate at the time of going to press. The publishers, however, cannot be held responsible for alterations, errors or omissions, but they would welcome notification of such for future editions.

Typeset in - Times - bold, italic and plain 9pt and 18pt.

Printed by - John N. Merrill at Milne House, Speedwell Mill, Miller's Green, Wirksworth, Derbyshire. DE4 4BL

Cover photograph by John N. Merrill - "Tower of Ulverscroft Priory". © Trail Crest Publications Ltd. 1992.

An all British product.

CONTENTS -

ABOUT JOHN N. MERRILL

John combines the characteristics and strength of a mountain climber with the stamina and athletic capabilities of a marathon runner. In this respect he is unique and has to his credit a whole string of remarkable long walks. He is without question the world's leading marathon walker.

Over the last twenty years he has walked more than 125,000 miles and successfully completed more than a dozen walks of a least 1,000 miles or more. His six major walks in Great Britain are
-

> Hebridean Journey....... 1,003 miles.
> Northern Isles Journey......913 miles.
> Irish Island Journey ....1,578 miles.
> Parkland Journey.......2,043 miles.
> Land's End to John o' Groats.....1,608 miles.

and in 1978 he became the first person to walk the entire coastline of Britain - 6,824 miles in ten months.

In Europe he has walked across Austria - 712 miles - hiked the Tour of Mont Blanc, completed High Level Routes in the Dolomites and Italian Alps, and the GR20 route across Corsica in training! Climbed the Tatra Mountains and walked in the Black Forest. He has walked across Europe - 2,806 miles in 107 days - crossing seven countries, the Swiss and French Alps and the complete Pyrennean chain - the hardest and longest mountain walk in Europe, with more than 600,000 feet of ascent!

In America he used The Appalachian Trail - 2,200 miles - as a training walk, before walking from Mexico to Canada via the Pacific Crest Trail in record time - 118 days for 2,700 miles. Recently he walked most of the Continental Divide Trail and much of New Mexico; his second home. In Canada he has walked the Rideau Trail - Kingston to Ottowa - 220 miles and The Bruce Trail - Tobermory to Niagara Falls - 460 miles.

John set off from Virginia Beach on the Atlantic coast, and walked 4,226 miles without a rest day, across the width of America to Santa Cruz and San Francisco on the Pacific coast. His walk is unquestionably his greatest achievement, being, in modern history, the longest, hardest crossing of the U.S.A. in the shortest time - under six months (178 days). The direct distance is 2,800 miles.

Between major walks John is out training in his own area - The Peak District National Park. He has walked all of our National Trails many times - The Cleveland Way thirteen times and The Pennine Way four times in a year! He has been trekking in the Himalayas five times. He created more than a dozen challenge walks which have been used to raise more than £300,000 for charity. From his own walks he has raised over £100,000. He is author of more than one hundred walking guides which he prints and publishes himself, His book sales are in excess of 2 1/2 million, He has created many long distance walks including The Limey Way , The Peakland Way, Dark Peak Challenge walk, and Rivers' Way.

INTRODUCTION

I first walked in the area in the late 1960's, when I was scarcely out of the pram! I remember staring with amazement at Mount St. Bernard Abbey and wandering around the ruins of Ulverscroft Priory, when it was owned by the then Ministry of Works. I little realised that it would be many years later that I would return and walk Bradgate Park again and explore more fully this "hilly" scenic area of north Leicestershire. Whilst the memories faded the key places remained unspoilt and I enjoyed many hours of discovering old paths and favourite haunts, as I revisited the area for a short circular walk guide. As I walked I began piecing together an idea of encircling the "forest" for a challenge walk.....this is the result!

After putting it off a couple of weekends I set off from Bradgate Park. The weather was fine - a cool June morning. The deer lay under the trees. I walked on through Newtown Linford and onto Ulverscroft before ascending to Copt Oak. The honeymoon was over, it was in the 90's! I pressed on to Bardon Hill and saw an army contingent on exercise, resting in the shade. Next I ascended to the Warren Hills and ignored the Bull's Head, thinking I could get something at Mount St. Bernard Abbey. I couldn't, so I carried on walking to Blackbrook Reservoir and onto the church in the Oaks of Charnwood. By the time I gained Beacon Hill, several miles later, I was really suffering from the heat. But at the bottom of the hill got an ice cream! A mile later in Woodhouse Eaves, I purchased 2 1/2 litres of milk and drank the lot! Feeling rather heavy I began the final miles to Swithland Wood and Bradgate Park as the temperature dropped. I would have to pick the hottest day of the year!

However, I entered the car park at Hall gates, delighted at the walk and the scenery and hills I had climbed. May I hope you have a fine day but not quite so hot, and enjoy the route around Charnwood Forest. Let me know how you got on and...

Happy walking!
John N. Merrill.
1992

HOW TO DO IT

The entire walk is covered by the 1:25,000 Pathfinder Series Map No. 874 (SK 41/51) - Loughborough (South).

The walk starts and ends at Hallgates car park in the north-eastern side of Bradgate Park, just off the B5330 near Cropston Reservoir at Grid Ref. SK543114.

The walk is in a clockwise direction and after 2 miles in Newtown Linford there are no real amenities, except the Copt Oak Inn at Copt Oak, 7 miles out and the Bull's Head Inn at Green Hill, 11 miles out, until you reach Woodhouse Eaves nearly 20 miles out. It is best to go self contained unless you have a back up party to meet you every few miles. Allow 8 to 10 hours to complete the walk. There is a Youth Hostel at Copt Oak and bed & breakfast and hotels in the Loughborough region - see amenities guide.

The country traversed is mostly gentle rolling hills with Bardon Hill being the steepest short ascent. Road walking is kept to a minimum but is necessary to link rights of way. The only long stretch - about 1 1/2 miles - is the B5330 to access the right of way onto Beacon Hill. There are few rights of way in the area and there is no alternative, but the Rippin Memorial Walk to Beacon Hill is a delight! The walk is a mixture of woodland and rocky summits with stunning views over Leicestershire and beyond. Newtown Linford and Woodhouse Eaves are most attractive villages.

For those who complete the circuit, there is a special four colour embroidered badge, illustrating a tree and a walking man, and a signed certificate available from Trail Crest Publications Ltd. They also keep a register of all the people who walk the route. An annual reunion of fellow walkers of John Merrill walks and challenges is held in late October each year.

Local weather information - Weathercall - 0898 500 412

Loughborough Tourist Information Centre -
John Storer House, Wards End,
Loughborough, Leicestershire.
LE11 3HA Tel. 0509 - 230131

ABOUT THE WALK

Whilst every care is taken detailing and describing the walk in this book, it should be borne in mind that the countryside changes by the seasons and the work of man. I have described the walk to the best of my ability, detailing what I have found on the walk in the way of stiles and signs. Obviously with the passage of time stiles become broken or replaced by a ladder stile or even a small gate. Signs too have a habit of being broken or pushed over. All the route follow rights of way and only on rare occasions will you have to overcome obstacles in its path, such as a barbed wire fence or electric fence. On rare occasions rights of way are rerouted and these ammendments are included in the next edition.

The seasons bring occasional problems whilst out walking which should also be borne in mind. In the height of summer paths become overgrown and you will have to fight your way through in a few places. In low lying areas the fields are often full of crops, and although the pathline goes straight across it may be more practical to walk round the field edge to get to the next stile or gate. In summer the ground is generally dry but in autumn and winter, especially because of our climate, the surface can be decidedly wet and slippery; sometimes even gluttonous mud!

These comments are part of countryside walking which help to make your walk more interesting or briefly frustrating. Standing in a farmyard up to your ankles in mud might not be funny at the time but upon reflection was one of the highlights of the walk!

The mileage for each walk is based on three calculations -

1. pedometer reading.
2. the route map measured on the map.
3. the time I took for the walk.

I believe the figure stated for each walk to be very accurate but we all walk differently and not always in a straight line! The time allowed for each walk is on the generous side and does not include pub stops etc. The figure is based on the fact that on average a person walks 2 1/2 miles an hours but less in hilly terrain.

View to Ulverscroft Priory - Stage one.

The Warren Hills - Stage two.

8

REMEMBER AND OBSERVE THE COUNTRY CODE

Enjoy the countryside and respect its life and work.

Guard against all risk of fire.

Fasten all gates.

Keep your dogs under close control.

Keep to public paths across farmland.

Use gates and stiles to cross fences, hedges and walls.

Leave livestock, crops and machinery alone.

Take your litter home - pack it in; pack it out.

Help to keep all water clean.

Protect wildlife, plants and trees.

Take special care on country roads

Make no unnecessary noise.

THE HIKER'S CODE

🌢 Hike only along marked routes - do not leave the trail.

🌢 Use stiles to climb fences; close gates.

🌢 Camp only in designated campsites.

🌢 Carry a light-weight stove.

🌢 Leave the trail cleaner than you found it.

🌢 Leave flowers and plants for others to enjoy.

🌢 Keep dogs on a leash.

🌢 Protect and do not disturb wildlife.

🌢 Use the trail at your own risk.

🌢 Leave only your thanks and footprints - take nothing but photographs.

STAGE ONE
BRADGATE PARK TO COPT OAK
- 7 MILES

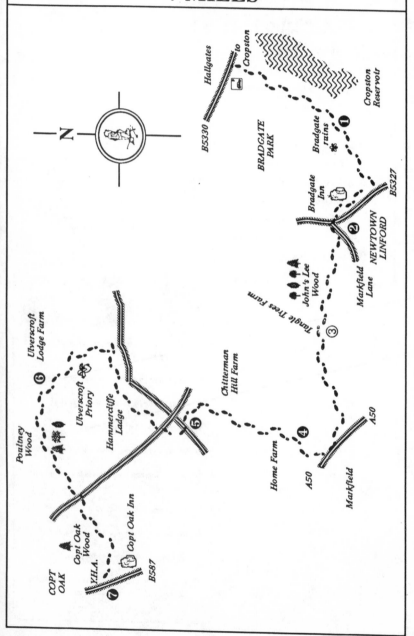

STAGE ONE - BRADGATE PARK TO COPT OAK - 7 MILES
- allow 2 1/2 hours

●● ●● ●● *- Hallgates - Bradgate Park - Newtown Linford - John's Lee Wood - Tangle Trees Farm - A50 - Home Farm - Chitterman Hill Farm - Ulverscroft Priory - Poultney Wood - Copt Oak.*

- 1:25,000 Pathfinder Series Sheet No. 874 (SK 41/51) - Loughborough (South).

- Hallgates, beside the B5330 in the N.E. corner of Bradgate Park. Grid Ref. SK543114.

- The Bradgate Inn and Bradgate Tea Room, Newtown Linford; Copt Oak Inn, Copt Oak.

ABOUT THE SECTION - Absolutely beautiful start through Bradgate Park, on a tarmaced track, past Cropston Reservoir, deer, Bradgate ruins, and tumbling weirs to Newtown Linford. The village is very picturesque with some stunning cottages. Following paths you cross the fields to the A50 before turning right and heading for Ulverscroft Priory. Here you ascend to Copt Oak and its Youth Hostel, ready for the hills ahead!

WALKING INSTRUCTIONS - Turn right out of the car park and through the kissing gate into Bradgate Park. Keep on this tarmaced track for 2 miles to car park at Newtown Linford. On the way passing Cropston Reservoir and deer on your left, then the ruins of Bradgate on your right, and on past the monument to Charles Bennion who in 1933 gave the park for the enjoyment of the people of Leicestershire. Continue on the path past the small waterfalls to the car park and Newtown Linford. Turn right and walk through the village along Bradgate Road then Main Street, past Bradgate Inn to the road junction. Turn left along Markfield Lane for a few yards to a stile and footpath sign on your right. The path crosses a field to the far righthand corner where there is a stile. Keep the field boundary on your right to the next stile; then it is on your left. Continue to another stile and keep the hedge on your right. Soon afterwards gain a track and walk just inside John Lee's Wood. Cross a farm drive to Tangle Trees Farm at the end of the wood, using stiles and bear right on a right of way across the field to the far righthand corner. The path is well signed with yellow topped posts, which together with the path sign of an outline of a foot, is a feature of walking in Charnwood Forest. The path keeps to the edge of the fields and beside Cover Cloud wood. Where the wood bears left is a yellow topped post, continue across the field to a stile and footbridge. Turn left then right around the field edge and onto a path by the A50 road.

Walk beside the road for 100 yards before turning right at stile and following the path past Home Farm on your left. The path is mostly a hedged one leading down and around to a footbridge. Continue ascending gently along the field edge past Chitterman Hill Farm to a lane. Turn left and at the crossroads turn right and descend past Hammercliffe Lodge to the track to Ulverscroft Priory 1/2 mile away. Turn left along the track past the priory. Just after the priory leave the track and follow a path along the field edge with Ulverscroft Pond on your left. Beyond the pond gain a stile with Ulverscroft Lodge Farm to your right. Soon afterwards bear left and cross a footbridge and walk through woodland and along a field edge to a gate. Continue to another and ascend through Poultney Wood to another gate. Continue along the field and woodland edge on your left to another gate. Continue ahead but soon leave the wood side and bear right to a stile. Continue along a fenced path to another stile and minor road. Turn left then right at the footpath sign - the climbing is now over for the moment. Keep to the field edge following a defined and well stiled path. To your left are communications masts. Follow the path round to your right to the church, dedicated to St. Peter, at Copt Oak. Gain the road with the inn/eating house on your left and the Youth Hostel on your right. Turn right to the road junction.

Charles Bennion plaque, Bradgate Park.

Bradgate ruins, Bradgate Park.

Waterfalls in Bradgate Park.

STAGE TWO
COPT OAK TO MOUNT ST. BERNARD ABBEY
- 6 MILES

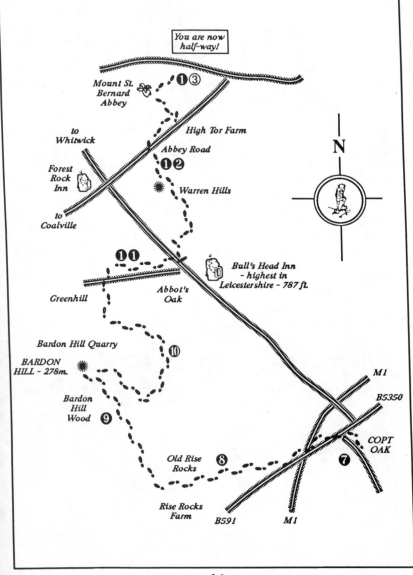

You are now half-way!

Mount St. Bernard Abbey

to Whitwick

High Tor Farm

Abbey Road

Forest Rock Inn

to Coalville

Warren Hills

N

Bull's Head Inn – highest in Leicestershire – 787 ft.

Greenhill

Abbot's Oak

Bardon Hill Quarry

BARDON HILL – 278m.

Bardon Hill Wood

Old Rise Rocks

Rise Rocks Farm

B591

M1

COPT OAK

M1

B5350

STAGE TWO - COPT OAK TO MOUNT ST. BERNARD ABBEY - 6 MILES
- allow 2 hours (minimum).

- Copt Oak - Old Rise Rocks - Bardon Hill Wood - Bardon Hill - Greenhill - Abbot's Oak - Warren Hills - High Tor Farm - Mount St. Bernard Abbey.

- 1:25,000 Pathfinder Series Sheet No. 874 - (SK 41/51) - Loughborough (South).

- Bull's Head Inn, Abbot's Oak - highest in Leicestershire - 787 feet.

ABOUT THE WALK - The main hilly section but delightful walking. First you cross the fields to Rise Rocks before heading northwards to the summit of Bardon Hill. From here you descend and walk through woodland to Greenhill and ascend to Abbot's Oak; just to the right of the route is the Bull's Head Inn, the highest in Leicestershire at 787 feet. You cross the Warren Hills before walking along the drive to the monastery, Mount St. Bernard Abbey. A really excellent stage and at the Abbey you are halfway!

WALKING INSTRUCTIONS - From the road junction at Copt Oak, turn left along the B591 road, crossing the M1. Just after the bridge, turn right and descend to a stile. Cross the next field to another stile and onto two more. Then keep the field boundary on your right, passing the Rise Rocks on your left and Old Rise Rocks house on your right. At the end of the field, just past the house, turn right - you are now loosely heading northwards to Mount St. Bernard Abbey. The path leads down keeping to the righthand side of the fields before rising to a small wood in the righthand corner of the second field. Here turn left then right at a stile and walk past the wood on your right. Ascend to a stile and avenue of trees. Cross to your right to a stile and continue to the right of a ruined farm. Walk past it and cross a track and continue on a defined path and ascend the wooded slopes of Bardon Hill. Pass the radio masts and continue along the "ridge" to the triangulation pillar and view down onto

15

Bardon Hill Quarry. Retrace your steps to the masts and descend the road for little over 1/4 mile. Where it turns right, turn left and follow the track along the edge of the woodland. In more than 1/2 mile the track turns right and follow it to the houses of Greenhill. Gaining the houses keep straight ahead along the road and alley ways to reach the minor road.

Turn right and ascend the road to Abbot's Oak and road junction. To your right is the Bull's Head Inn. Turn left and in a few yards turn right at the stile and footpath sign. Ascend the wide path to the top and turn left keeping the wall on your right and follow the path over the Warren Hills. In more than 1/2 mile reach Abbey Road. Turn right and about 100 yards later just before High Tor Farm, turn left and go through the gate onto the drive to Mount S. Bernard Abbey. Follow the drive round to your right and past the abbey to the road.

MOUNT ST. BERNARD ABBEY - The abbey was opened in 1835 and is the first Catholic Abbey in this country following the Reformation. The monks are of the Cistercian Order. The abbey is open to the public and well worth visiting.

Thatched cottage in Nowtown Linford.

IN
REMEMBRANCE OF
FREDERICK WILLIAM
FOWKES
1897 – 1987
AND
MARY MATILDA
FOWKES
1895 – 1991

Her baking's done.
His plants are left.
Their home is far behind.
A miner and his wife have gone,
A better place to find.

Gravestone in Copt Oak churchyard - on your left as you enter.

STAGE THREE
MOUNT ST. BERNARD ABBEY TO
BEACON HILL - 5 MILES

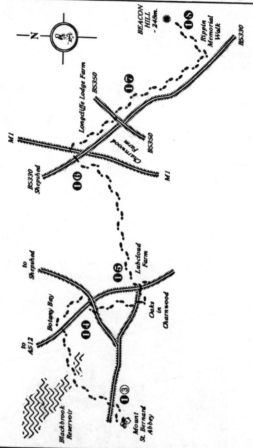

- from opposite page -

righthand side to a gate and continue ascending on a grass track. At the top of the field is a gate and turn right to another. Then left along the field edge to another and continue on a track to a farm building. Turn left to reach a gate and B5330 road. Turn right and pass under the M1. Keep on the road past Longcliffe Lodge Farm on your left and Charnwood Farm on your right to a cross roads. Cross over and keep on this road for a mile, as it descends then ascends towards Beacon Hill. After a mile turn left through a stile by a path sign and walk up the Rippin Memorial Walk, along an avenue of trees. At the top turn right then left to the rocks of Beacon Hill. The triangulation pillar is just ahead. The next part of the route is along the main track to your left.

STAGE THREE
MOUNT ST.
BERNARD ABBEY
TO BEACON HILL
- 5 MILES
- allow 1 3/4 hours.

- *Mount St. Bernard Abbey - Blackbrook Reservoir - Botany Bay - Oaks in Charnwood - Lubcloud Farm - M1 - Longcliffe Lodge Farm - B5330 - Beacon Hill.*

- *1:25,000 Pathfinder Series Sheet No. 874 - (SK 41/51) - Loughborough (South).*

- *nothing! Ice cream van at Beacon Hill car park, during summer months.*

ABOUT THE WALK - First you descend and cross Blackbrook Reservoir - a particularly attractive feature - before following lanes and paths to Oaks in Charnwood. Here you cross the fields to pass under the M1 before road walking to the Rippin Memorial Walk onto Beacon Hill. You are now over half-way......it is all downhill now!

WALKING INSTRUCTIONS - From the drive entrance to Mount St. Bernard Abbey, turn right along the road for a few yards to the path sign and stile on your left. Turn left and descend the field and woodland to another and a track. Cross over and continue descending with views of Blackbrook Reservoir to a stile. Turn right and soon left to cross the bridge over the reservoir; perhaps seeing grey herons. Continue along the track to the minor road at Botany Bay, little over 1/4 mile away. Turn right to the cross roads 1/4 mile away. Turn right and ascend the road - Abbey Road - for less than 1/4 mile. Look for a kissing gate on your left. Go through this and keep the field boundary on your right to reach two stiles. Descend the next field to a kissing gate, path sign, and road. Turn left passing the tennis club on your right and the church in the hamlet of Oaks in Charnwood dedicated to St. James the creator, on your left.

Follow the road to a T junction and turn left and in a few yards turn right at the bridlepath sign and ascend the track to Lubcloud Farm. Walk through the
- continued opposite -

19

STAGE FOUR -
BEACON HILL TO BRADGATE PARK
- 7 MILES

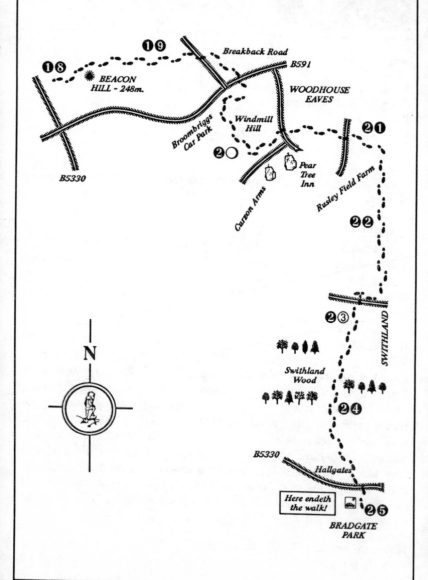

STAGE FOUR - BEACON HILL TO BRADGATE PARK - 7 MILES
- allow 2 1/2 hours.

- Beacon Hill - Breakback Road - Windmill Hill - Woodhouse Eaves - Rushley Field Farm - Swithland - Swithland Wood - Hallgates - Bradgate Park.

- 1:25,000 Pathfinder Series Sheet No. 874 - (SK 41/51) - Loughborough (South)

- Curzon Arms and Pear Tree Inn, Woodhouse Eaves.

ABOUT THE WALK - The final few miles - nearly all downhill! You descend Beacon Hill with views of Loughborough and beyond before ascending Windmill Hill. Just after you enter Woodhouse Eaves your first village for 18 miles, with shops to satisfy your appetite and thirst. Leaving the attractive village you cross fields to near Swithland and enter Swithland Wood before gaining Hallgates and the car park where you began 8 or 10 hours ago.

WALKING INSTRUCTIONS - From Beacon Hill follow the wide track on the lefthand side of the hill (northern side) and descend through woodland and rhoderdendrons to the car park at its eastern end. Gain the road - Breakback Road - and turn right. At the end of the road, 1/4 mile later, turn right and in about 100 yards turn left at the stile by Broombrigge car park. The path leads straight ahead over Windmill Hill and down into Mill Road. Follow it down into Woodhouse Eaves. Turn left along the road past the Curzon Arms on your right, to the road junction with the Pear Tree Inn on your right. Cross over to your right and walk along Meadow Road and opposite St. Paul's School turn right through the gate and follow the path across the field to a lane 1/2 mile away. Cross over to a stile and path sign and keep to the field edge on your left to a track. Turn right up the farm track towards Rushley Field Farm. Approaching the farm turn right over the wooden fence and cross the field to the right of the houses to a stile, footpath sign, and lane. Turn left along it for a few yards to a stile and footpath sign on your right.

The path keeps to the field edge to a stile then cross towards the righthand side of the next field to a footbridge. Cross this and keep the field hedge on your left for the next three fields to a stile and road on the outskirts of Swithland. Turn right and in 100 yards just after Woodland Cottage, turn left along a track/path and enter Swithland Wood. Basically keep ahead at all junctions and in 3/4 mile pass a fence, surrounding a quarry lake on your right. Continue on the defined track and just before crossing a bridge turn left along the wood's edge to a stile and footbridge. Cross this and cross the field on a defined path to a stile and footpath sign - "Swithland" at Hallgates. Turn left along the road and in a few strides on your right is the car-park where you began. Here is journey's end and may I be the first to congratulate you on successfully completing the route - *WELL DONE!*

Houses, Woodhouse Eaves.

Blackbrook Reservoir.

Beacon Hill.

AMENITIES GUIDE -

INNS -
The Bradgate Inn, Newtown Linford.
Copt Oak Inn, Copt Oak.
Bull's Head Inn, Abbot's Bromley.
Curzon Arms, Pear Tree Inn, Woodhouse Eaves

FARMHOUSE ACCOMODATION - not on the route
The Uplands Farm, Long Whatton, Nr. Loughborough, Leics. LE12 5DN.
Tel. 0509-842244.
Talbot House Farm, Thringstone, Coalville, Leicestershire. LE6 4NQ. Tel.
0530-222233.

YOUTH HOSTEL -
Copt Oak, Markfield, Leicestershire. LE6 0QB. Tel. 0530-242661

HALLGATES - 280 FT.

PRIORY LANE - 550 FT.

ULVERSCROFT - 500 FT.

COPT OAK - 709 FT.

BARDON HILL - 912 FT.

GREENHILL - 675 FT.

WARREN HILLS - 780 FT.

BLACKBROOK - 450 FT.

LUBCLOUD - 600 FT.

BEACON HILL - 818 FT.

HALLGATES - 280 FT.

CHARNWOOD FOREST

TRAIL PROFILE - approx - 1,600 feet of ascent and descent, over 25 miles

LOG

DATE STARTED...

DATE COMPLETED...

ROUTE POINT	MILE NO.	ARR.	DEP.	COMMENTS WEATHER
Hallgates	0			
Bradgate - ruins	1			
Newtown Linford	2			
A50	4			
Ulverscroft Priory	6			
Copt Oak	7			
Bardon Hill	9			
Warren Hills	11.5			
Mt.St.Bernard Abb.	12.5			
Blackbrook Res.	13.5			
M1	16			
Beacon Hill	18			
Woodhouse Eaves	20			
Swithland Wood	23			
Hallgates	25			

JOHN MERRILL'S CHARNWOOD FOREST CHALLENGE WALK

Badges measure 3 1/2" wide by 3" high and are a green cloth with brown, black, yellow and white embroidery.

BADGE ORDER FORM

Date completed ....

Time ....

Name..

Address ....

....

Price - £2.50 each including postage, VAT and signed certificate.

"I've done a John Merrill Walk" T shirt - Emerald Green with white lettering - all sizes - £7.50 including postage and VAT.

From - Trail Crest Publications Ltd., Winster, Matlock, Derbyshire. DE4 2DQ
TEL. Winster - 0629 - 650454 (24 hrs.)
.... **You may photocopy this form if needed** ....

THE JOHN MERRILL CHALLENGE WALK BADGE - walk this route twice or complete another of John Merrill's Challenge Walks and send details and cheque for £2.50 for a special 2 challenge walk circular four colour embroidered badge, to Trail Crest Publications; Ltd. price includes postage and VAT.

This is to certify that

....

has walked 25 miles around Charnwood Forest - over rocky hills, through woodland, and past monastic ruins following John Merrill's

CHARNWOOD FOREST CHALLENGE WALK

on

....

Signed

John N. Merrill

OTHER CHALLENGE WALKS BY JOHN N. MERRILL

DAY CHALLENGES -

John Merrill's White Peak Challenge Walk - 25 miles.
Circular walk from Bakewell involving 3,600 feet of ascent.

John Merrill's Dark Peak Challenge Walk - 24 miles.
Circular walk from Hathersage involving 3,300 feet of ascent.

**John Merrill's Staffordshire Moorlands Challenge Walk
- 26 miles.** Circular walk from Oakamoor involving 2,200 feet of ascent.

John Merrill's Yorkshire Dales Challenge Walk - 23 miles.
Circular walk from Kettlewell involving 3,600 feet of ascent.

John Merrill's North Yorkshire Moors Challenge Walk - 24 miles.
Circular walk from Goathland - a seaside bash - involving 2,000 feet of ascent.

The Little John Challenge Walk - 28 miles.
Circular walk from Edwinstowe in Sherwood Forest - Robin Hood
country.

Peak District End to End Walks.
1. Gritstone Edge Walk - 23 miles down the eastern edge system.
2. Limestone Dale Walk - 24 miles down the limestone dales from
Buxton to Ashbourne.

The Rutland Water Challenge walk - 24 miles
Around the shore of Rutland Water, the largest man made reservoir in Britain.

The Malvern Hills Challenge Walk - 20 miles.
Beneath and along the crest of the Malvern Hills.

The Salter's Way - 25 miles.
Across Cheshire from Northwich to the Pennines, following an old salt way.

John Merrill's Snowdon Challenge Walk - 30 miles.
A tough day walk involving 5,000 feet of ascent and descent from the sea to the
summit of Snowdon AND BACK!

John Merrill's Charnwood Forest Challenge Walk - 25 miles

The grandslam of this area of north Leicestershire, starting from Bradgate Park, taking in several hill's and monastic buildings, involving 1,600 feet of ascent and descent

Forthcoming titles -
John Merrill's Three Counties Challenge Walk.
The Quantock's Way.

MULTIPLE DAY CHALLENGE WALKS -

The Limey Way - 40 miles
Down twenty limestone dales from Castleton to Thorpe in the Peak District in eight stages, starting and ending at Ashbourne. The finest longest distance walk in the Peak! Taking in the grandest and highest sights.

The River's Way - 43 miles.
Down the five main river systems of the Peak District, from Edale, the end of the Pennine Way, to Ilam.

The Peakland Way - 96 miles.
John Merrill's classic walk around the Peak District National Park, starting and finishing at Ashbourne. The route of eight stages takes in the variety of the Park - limestone dales, gritstone moorland, gritstone edges , historic buildings and trails. A route combing the finest assets the Peak District has. More than 7,000 people have walked the entire route since it was inugurated in 1974.

Peak District High Level Route - 90 miles
Clrcular walk from Matlock taking in the highest and remotest parts of the Peak District.

COASTAL WALKS & NATIONAL TRAILS -

The Cleveland Way - 112 miles around the North Yorkshire Moors and coast
- a truly exceptional walk.

The Isle of Wight Coast Path - 77 miles.
Complete encirclement of a magnificent island.

Forthcoming titles -
Walking Angelsey's coastline.
The Pembrokeshire Coast Path.
The Ridgeway
Offa's Dyke Path

The Pilgrim's Way
The North Downs Way
The South Downs Way

"from footprint to finished book"

OTHER BOOKS by John N. Merrill Published by TRAIL CREST PUBLICATIONS Ltd.

CHARNWOOD FOREST CHALLENGE WALK

INSTRUCTION & RECORD -
HIKE TO BE FIT.....STROLLING WITH JOHN
THE JOHN MERRILL WALK RECORD BOOK

MULTIPLE DAY WALKS -
THE RIVERS'S WAY
PEAK DISTRICT: HIGH LEVEL ROUTE
PEAK DISTRICT MARATHONS
THE LIMEY WAY
THE PEAKLAND WAY

COAST WALKS & NATIONAL TRAILS -
ISLE OF WIGHT COAST PATH
PEMBROKESHIRE COAST PATH
THE CLEVELAND WAY

PEAK DISTRICT HISTORICAL GUIDES -
A to Z GUIDE OF THE PEAK DISTRICT
DERBYSHIRE INNS - an A to Z guide
HALLS AND CASTLES OF THE PEAK DISTRICT & DERBYSHIRE
TOURING THE PEAK DISTRICT & DERBYSHIRE BY CAR
DERBYSHIRE FOLKLORE
PUNISHMENT IN DERBYSHIRE
CUSTOMS OF THE PEAK DISTRICT & DERBYSHIRE
WINSTER - a souvenir guide
ARKWRIGHT OF CROMFORD
LEGENDS OF DERBYSHIRE
TALES FROM THE MINES by Geoffrey Carr
PEAK DISTRICT PLACE NAMES by Martin Spray

JOHN MERRILL'S MAJOR WALKS -
TURN RIGHT AT LAND'S END
WITH MUSTARD ON MY BACK
TURN RIGHT AT DEATH VALLEY
EMERALD COAST WALK

COLOUR GUIDES -
THE PEAK DISTRICT.........Something to remember her by.

SKETCH BOOKS -
NORTH STAFFORDSHIRE SKETCHBOOK by John Creber
SKETCHES OF THE PEAK DISTRICT

IN PREPARATION -
SHORT CIRCULAR WALKS IN THE YORKSHIRE DALES - Vol 1. - Southern area.
SHORT CIRCULAR WALKS IN THE LAKE DISTRICT
SHORT CIRCULAR WALKS IN NORTH YORKSHIRE MOORS
FOOTPATHS OF THE WORLD - Vol 1 - NORTH AMERICA
HIKING IN NEW MEXICO - 7 VOLUMES
Vol I - The Sandia and Manzano Mountains.

☞ **Full list from TRAIL CREST PUBLICATIONS Ltd.,**
Winster, Matlock, Derbyshire. DE4 2DQ